This Book Belongs To:

____

BY
Home Planners And
Journals

To help you organize your life

This book is copyright protected. Reproducing this book is prohibited and not allowed without the permission of the author. All rights reserved.

9 781796 512380